JUST ANOTHER GUIDE TO ETHICAL HACKING

PAVAN KUMAR

XpressPublishing
An imprint of Notion Press

XpressPublishing
An imprint of Notion Press

Old No. 38, New No. 6
McNichols Road, Chetpet
Chennai - 600 031

First Published by Notion Press 2019
Copyright © Pavan Kumar 2019
All Rights Reserved.

ISBN 978-1-64678-449-3

To,

my parents for their constant love and support

my best friend, Preeth

Contents

Acknowledgements

Much obliged to all whose help, care and inspiration helped me and prodded me on in the composition of this book. I am particularly thankful to my family for their support and attentive words that consistently came at the correct time, giving the required drive to make this book a triumph. For the profitable assistance they rendered from my adolescence up to this point and all through this task, I truly appreciate. Their help and love propped me up - guaranteeing I never considered yielding until my point was accomplished. They are the best accomplices I can ever dream of and they have given me their closest to perfect!

CHAPTER ONE

Introduction

Everybody who chips away at a PC must be acquainted with the expression "Digital Crime." Initially, when man developed PC and afterward the innovation for conveying between PCs was advanced, he would have never felt that the internet he is making could be overwhelmed with any wrongdoing for example digital wrongdoing. Be that as it may, presently practically we all may have heard the term PC wrongdoing, digital wrongdoing, e-wrongdoing, hello there tech wrongdoing or electronic wrongdoing which is only an action finished with a criminal aim in the internet. Basically, it is an action which is criminal in nature, where a PC or system is the source, device, target, or spot of a wrongdoing. To state in one line, "Digital wrongdoing alludes to every one of the exercises finished with criminal expectation in the internet."

Why, think about Cyber Crime?

The greater part of us are utilizing web and PCs for online exchanges where we transmit individual data and conceivably do financial exchanges. In the event that your own data goes in an inappropriate hands and you become bankrupt or you start accepting crazy sends or your email record gets overwhelmed with undesirable sends; implies you have turned into a casualty of Cyber Crime.

The programmer's primary point is to upset a framework or system. Regardless of whether he is a white hat programmer or dark hat programmer his degree of pulverization is to stop or get the entrance to the PC frameworks. Continued hacking or altering continually may take a programmer in jail yet commonly these wrongdoings are messed with.

What is Hacking?

What is your meaning of hacking? A great many people think about the news stories that identify with huge undertakings having humiliating issues as their information is undermined. In any case, in truth, hacking goes a part more remote than this.

PC hacking is the act of causing noxious changes to a program so as to accomplish an objective outside the first motivation behind the maker. An individual who connects with into these exercises is known as a Hacker, who is a typically a specialist software engineer who sees hacking as a craftsmanship and as an approach to apply their aptitudes, all things considered, circumstances. Yet, different programmers have unquestionably more perilous destinations than just to show their abilities, such as taking individual data, increasing unapproved access to.

It doesn't generally need to be somebody you don't have the foggiest idea who hacks into your frameworks and causes issues for your business. It could really be somebody who works for you that doesn't have your eventual benefits on a basic level. This is on the grounds that the essential significance of hacking is the point at which somebody gets to a few or the majority of your PC frameworks without consent. Furthermore, it doesn't simply occur over the web.

Frequently, numerous individuals don't perceive how boundless PC hacking can be. Expecting that they are just in threat from web based assaults implies they may not be secured for all dangers. Indeed, even those organizations that do everything they can to anticipate hacking which happens online may have accidentally chosen not to see different risks.

This is the explanation an appreciation of what hacking is and what it incorporates can help you with ensuring your very own business even more totally. In any case, what do you do in case you don't have the foggiest thought regarding all of the unpredictable subtleties of the risks displayed?

The least requesting plan is to rely upon a master to guarantee every potential opening is halted, and no one can break into your systems. Framework invasion testing is maybe the best ways to deal with see how incredible your PC organize genuinely is. If you do have vulnerabilities it's optimal to find by methods for someone who is clear and is looking for them to benefit you. In case you expect everything is great and it isn't, you could be in for a terrible paralyze at some point or another.

An expert in the field of moral hacking would have the choice to highlight any potential issues and settle them before some other individual got a chance to mishandle them. Likewise, that is most likely an organization that justifies paying for.

Try not to tragically think this should just be done once however. Programmers are continually finding new ways into beforehand secure frameworks. In the event that you utilize an organization to perceive how cutting-edge your safety efforts truly are, ensure you do it all the time. In the event that you don't, regardless you risk being gotten out.

Moral programmers expect to bring into the manager's notice, vulnerabilities and voids in the framework in this manner. They are absolutely tech-nerds with faultless programming abilities and hands-on information on both PC equipment and programming. Then again, there are individuals who can however break into frameworks, gain admittance to verified records yet their activities are generally unapproved while they make a secondary passage section into your framework. These individuals (frequently misconstrued as programmers) are called as 'wafers. They attempt and break passwords, security codes, and so forth utilizing different hacking programming's which are as of now accessible. Such programming are intended to break the code utilizing a large number of preliminaries modified into it by different programmers.

Cyber Threats:

Taken information are circled as against the licensed innovation laws as indicated by such belief system dangers. These crooks see themselves as Robin Hood and spread the information which is protected under licensed innovation rights. Numerous psychological militant exercises are likewise named as belief system dangers in the digital world. They spread their very own belief system or contradict government's by utilizing the web innovation. Their essential point is to cover their belief system or standards and contradicting what is against their exercises. Numerous fear based oppressors' arrangements and information's are additionally considered as digital dangers.

In this way whatever be the idea of digital wrongdoing exacting laws must be controlled to empower a verified the internet. As increasingly more of our day by day exercises winds up associated or interlinked in the internet the requirement for a total secure innovation has turned into the need of great importance. Regardless of whether it is basic email hacking or phishing, the individuals engaged with such exercises are certainly attacking the security of people and business associations. Personality burglaries, cash cheating, and charge card tricks are grave issues which can make unsalvageable harm the individual concerned.

Customary digital wrongdoings

Lawbreakers whose emphasis is on financial increases just are called conventional digital culprits. The greater part of them are distinguished as some inside source. Ongoing investigation has affirmed to practically 80% wrongdoers of such violations have a place with organization or firm. Mechanical secret activities, scholarly legitimate wrongdoing, trademark infringement, illicit reserve moves, and so on are a portion of the conventional digital violations. Such offenders who direct these violations are bound to wind up in the slammer if the wrongdoing is demonstrated.

CHAPTER TWO

Essentials for a hacker

Step 1: Learn To Program in C

C writing computer programs being one of the most dominant dialects in PC programming, It is important to truly ace this language. This programming language was designed by Denise Ritchie in the middle of the years 1969 and 1973 at AT&T Bell Labs. C programming will basically enable you to isolate the assignment in littler pieces and these pieces can be communicated by an arrangement of directions. Give thinking of some program a shot your own by evaluating the rationale.

Step 2: Learn More Than One Programming Language

When you are attempting to turn into a programmer, it is imperative to learn other present day PC programming dialects, for example, JAVA, Perl, PHP, and Python. Perhaps the most ideal approaches to get familiar with these is by perusing books from specialists. It will likewise think about markup dialects like XML, HTML and information organizations, for example, Json, Protobuf and others which are basic approach to move information among customer and server.

- Java is one of the most well-known programming dialects. It has been guaranteed that it's additionally extremely secure. Knowing Java security model will engage you to see how this language accomplishes security. Find out about the security escape clauses in Java language and related structures. Pick and read from many free PDF, instructional exercises and eBooks accessible to learn java on the web.

- Perl is a broadly useful powerful programming language, which is a significant level and can be translated. This language obtains a few highlights of C language. Then again, JAVA is simultaneous, class-based and articles arranged programming language. Python is extremely convenient when you are attempting to computerize some dreary errands.

- HTML is the markup language dependent on which the site pages are structured, made and showed. The internet browsers read the HTML code to show the website page.

- Python is the best language for web improvement and most loved language of a part of the developer because of its effortlessness and fast turnaround. Many individuals use Python to do straightforward and complex computerization.

Stage 3: Learn UNIX

UNIX is performing multiple tasks and multi-client PC working framework that is intended to give great security to the frameworks. This working framework was created by certain representatives of AT&T in Bell Labs. The most ideal approach to learn it is to get into an open-source adaptation (for example cent OS) and introduce/run the equivalent all alone. You can work web without learning UNIX, yet it isn't feasible for you to be a web programmer without getting UNIX.

On the off chance that you have not utilized UNIX working framework yet, a couple of basic Linux directions will make your agreeable in kicking rapidly off.

An enormous number of web servers are facilitated on UNIX based servers and knowing internals of this working framework will be extremely a major lift in your abilities.

Stage 4: Learn More Than One Operating Systems

There are numerous other working frameworks separated from UNIX. Windows working framework is one of the most generally traded off frameworks, thus it is a great idea to pick up hacking Microsoft frameworks, which are shut source frameworks.

As indicated by the National Vulnerability Database, Microsoft working frameworks have countless vulnerabilities.

Windows OS installers are disseminated in parallel, in this manner it is difficult for you to peruse the code. Double code is the computerized portrayal of content and information that the PC gets it. Be that as it may, realizing how projects are composed for windows and how various applications to act on this working framework will help.

One of the ongoing vulnerabilities of a mainstream OS was that Java Web Start applications get propelled naturally regardless of whether the Java modules are impaired. Turning into a programmer is tied in with knowing the shortcomings of these working frameworks and focusing on them methodically.

Stage 5: Learn Networking Concepts

The systems administration idea should be sharp when you need to be a programmer.

Seeing how the systems are made is significant, any way you have to know the contrasts between various kinds are systems. Having an unmistakable comprehension of TCP/

IP and UDP convention is an unquestionable requirement to have the option to abuse the vulnerabilities on the World Wide Web.

Comprehend what subnet, LAN, WAN is and VPN.

The systems administration directions to do an HTTP solicitation should be on your fingertips. The HTTP convention is the door through which one enters the web world, consequently, it is important to get familiar with this convention so as to break the hindrances. The programmers regularly utilize the HTTP portal to rupture the security of the framework and assume responsibility for it.

Apache Httpd is one of the most ordinarily utilized web servers and knowing all through it will enable you on any HTTP or other application layer convention-related undertakings.

Nmap is a ground-breaking system checking device that is utilized by programmers and security proficient over the world to recognize defenseless has. In any case, to viably begin utilizing it you should comprehend the systems administration essentials. To get propelled abilities on Nmap you can allude the book by makers - Nmap Network Scanning: The Official Nmap Project Guide to Network Discovery and Security Scanning

Stage 6: Start Simple: Read Some Tutorials about Hacking

This is the basic and most ideal approach to begin. Peruse whatever number instructional exercises as would be prudent that are intended for hacking. These articles will give you understanding and help you build up the demeanor to be a programmer. A few instructional exercises will start you with Nmap, Nessus and SuperScan, a portion of the hacking projects or apparatuses that programmers for the most part use. These instructional exercises are promptly accessible over the web; both content and video instructional exercises are accessible for you to respond to your inquiry on how to be a programmer.

Stage 7: Learn Cryptography

As a specialist programmer, you have to comprehend and ace the specialty of cryptography. The innovation of cryptography and encryption is significant for web and Networking. It is the training and investigation of strategies that are utilized for secure correspondence within the sight of the outsiders. The encryption is accomplished for different parts of data security, for example, privacy of the information, trustworthiness of the information and confirmation. In addition, the innovation of cryptography is broadly utilized in ATM cards, PC passwords and internet business. While hacking, these encrypted codes should be broken, which is called unscrambling.

Cryptography is intensely utilized in SSL based web correspondence. A master programmer ought to have the option to see how SSL functions and what is the significance of cryptography in keeping SSL secure.

Comprehend different strategies utilized for secret phrase splitting,

There are many devices accessible to do secret key splitting, and utilizing it isn't hacking. To be master at hacking it's significant for you to see how to make a program that can break a secret word from figure content.

Stage 8: Experiment A Lot

This is a significant advance for setting yourself up as a specialist programmer. Arrangement a research center alone to explore the learning on the functional applications. A least difficult lab will have your PC, anyway once you advance you might need to include an ever-increasing number of PCs and required equipment for your trials.

It is great to take a stab at investigating your own PCs, where you can amend in the event that you have done any misstep. Numerous programmers at first start off by downloading virtual lab applications, for example, Oracle Virtual Box. You require at any rate 3 GBs of RAM and a nearly amazing processor to complete your hacking tests. Setting up the virtual machine is vital, as it will enable you to test infection, applications, and various servers without influencing your own PC.

A portion of the things you may need to remember when doing tests

- Document your progress.
- Keep improvising.
- Automate repetitive tasks.
- Keep a backup before any experiment i.e. a screenshot if you are doing it in a virtual lab environment.
- Start small and have checkpoints.
- Know when to stop.

CHAPTER THREE

Phases of hacking

Hacking is separated into five stages: Reconnaissance, Scanning, Gaining Access, Maintaining Access, lastly clearing tracks. The more you draw near to all stages, the more stealth will be your assault

1. Reconnaissance: This is the essential stage where the programmer attempts to gather however much data as could be expected about the objective. It incorporates recognizing the objective, discovering the objective IP address extend, organize, area name enrollment records of the objective, mail server records, DNS records.

2. Scanning: This makes up the base of hacking! This is the place getting ready for assault really starts! After surveillance the assailant examines the objective for administrations running, open ports, firewall discovery, discovering vulnerabilities, working framework recognition.

3. Access: After examining, the programmers structures the diagram of the system of the objective with the assistance of stuffs gathered during stages one and 21 Now, the aggressor, executes the assault dependent on the vulnerabilities which were distinguished during filtering! After the effective assault, he gains admittance to the objective network!!!! So cool!! He is currently, the lord!!!

4. Maintaining Access: After obtaining entrance, the assailant raises the benefits to root/administrator and transfers a bit of code normally called as secondary passage) on the objective system with the goal that he generally keep up the got entrance and can associate with objective whenever!

5. Covering Track: After getting entrance and keeping up the equivalent, programmer abuses the shortcoming and hacks the system or abuses the entrance! From that point onward, comes the significant stage covering the tracks! To abstain from getting followed and captured, programmer clears every one of the tracks by clearing a wide range of logs and erased the transferred secondary passage and anything related stuff which may later mirror his quality! So these are five significant periods of hacking which each programmer must pursue for a fruitful assault!

Security and Privacy

We are largely now very much aware of the dangers confronting PCs, for example, DDoS assaults against servers, what precisely a zombie PC is and a few hacks which have hit the papers - like the tale of a man in Tampa Bay who was found taking another person's broadband association. The individual hacked into a remote web organize. While this may appear to be blameless enough think about that the individual who additions section into the system could be utilizing your association with surf for pornography - or more terrible it could be child pornography, with the trail prompting your association.

Indeed you may need to have your very own specialists helping you demonstrate your guiltlessness!

Another comparable story of broadband/remote sign burglary from out of the UK, where a few people have been charged utilizing another person's broadband association.

While the fines have been heavy, it is an unmistakable sign that while the equity framework Is moving in the direction of ensuring people, they are in a strange area. On the off chance that you have ever acquired another person's remote association - you should reconsider. On the off chance that the stated aim of the law is pursued, you could wind up with genuine fines, prison time - and more awful, a record that will tail you forever.

On the off chance that you have a remote web association in your home, or office - secure it! In addition to the fact that you are ensuring yourself, your business and its benefits - however you could be keeping somebody from propelling obliterating assaults against business frameworks, or enabling fear based oppressors from utilizing open frameworks to speak with others and notwithstanding halting the progression of kid sex entertainment.

Disregard what should be possible utilizing your remote association - think about that a considerable lot of us store our whole lives on our computers: digital pictures, films, banking data, and even e-bills. In the event that somebody gets unapproved access to your PC, you hazard having your personality taken. You have to guarantee your PCs are adequately verified to anticipate unapproved access to its substance.

CHAPTER FOUR

Types of hacking

Hacking is usually meant to break a code. There are three sections of hacking which are Web Hacking, Exploit Writing & Reverse Engineering and each of it requires different programming language.

1. Web Hacking

Since the majority of the tech is worked around the World Wide Web, it is essential to learn web hacking to be a decent programmer. Suppose you are keen on hacking web applications as well as sites then you should learn web coding. Sites use for the most part HTML, PHP, and JavaScript so it is critical to gain proficiency with these three.

- **HTML:**

One of the most straightforward and generally utilized static markup web language present in every single site you find in your program. It's prescribed to learn HTML since it helps understanding web activities, reaction, and rationale.

- **JavaScript:**

JS is a customer side web programming for the most part utilized in sites for better UI and snappy reaction. On the off chance that you are keen on a hacking vocation you have to learn JavaScript on the grounds that it comprehends customer side system which is basic for discovering customer side imperfections.

• **PHP:**

A unique server-side language which is in charge of overseeing web-applications and database. PHP is viewed as one of the most basic languages since it controls everything on location and server, similar to a commander of a ship. It is encouraged to learn PHP pleasantly.

• **SQL:**

SQL is in charge of putting away and overseeing touchy and classified information, for example, client qualifications, bank and individual data about the site guests. Dark cap programmers generally target SQL database and take data which are later sold on underground dull web gathering. On the off chance that you need to be a great security scientist, you ought to learn SQL with the goal that you can discover imperfections in a site and report them.

2. Exploit Writing

After web hacking, another most significant element of hacking is abused. You can break specific programming by writing an exploit. Be that as it may, to write an exploit you have to adapt either Python or Ruby.

• **Python:**

It is said that a security specialist or programmer should know Python since it the center language for writing exploits and apparatuses. Security specialists and even expert programmers propose that ace Python is the most ideal approach to get the hang of hacking. Python offers more extensive adaptability and you can make misuses just in the event that you are great in Python.

- **Ruby:**

Figuring out, the way toward taking a product program's double code and reproducing it in order to follow it back to the first source code. In the event that you know figuring out, you can discover imperfections and bugs effectively. In the event that you need to learn figuring out you have to know C, C++ and Java. The way toward changing over the code written in significant level language into a low level language without changing the first program is known as figuring out.

CHAPTER FIVE

Best hacking tools

1. Nmap

System Mapper is free and popular open source developer's gadget. lt is basically used for divulgence and security assessing. lt is being used by a large number of structure chiefs over the world with the ultimate objective of framework stock, survey open ports administer organization update, plan similarly as to look at host or organization uptime. There are a couple of focal points of using Network Mapper, one among its inclinations is that the overseer customer can screen whether the framework and related center points require fixing.

2. Acutenix (Web Vulnerability Scanner):

Acutenix Web Vulnerability Scanner consequently slithers your site and it naturally screens your web applications and distinguishes perilous SQL infusion. It likewise figures out where applications should be verified, in this way shielding your business from programmers.

3. Metasploit:

Metasploit Project is an incredibly renowned hacking structure or pentesting. lt is a lot of hacking apparatuses that are utilized to execute various assignments. This device is fundamentally utilized by Cyber security experts and moral programmers. Metasploit is a PC security venture or structure which gives the client important data about security vulnerabilities.

4.0wasp Zed Attack Proxy Project:

ZAP and is condensed as Zed Attack Proxy is among famous OWASP Projects. It is exceptionally incredible and simple to utilize apparatus that discovers vulnerabilities in Web Applications. It is the moderately prevalent device due to its help and OWASP people group. OWASP people group is sublime asset for those individuals that work inside Cyber Security.

5. Wireshark

Wireshark is organize analyzer which allows the analyzer to catch bundles moving through the system and to screen it. Wireshark has been for drawn out time, and it is presently being utilized by a great many security experts to look at systems and investigate for snag and interruptions.

6. Burp Suite

Burp Suite is arrange helplessness scanner, especially with some propelled highlights. There are two ordinarily utilized applications with this apparatus which includes 'Burp Suite Spider' which can rundown and guide out the various pages and parameters of a site by investigating treats. It is significant device on the off chance that you are taking a shot at digital security.

7. THC Hydra

THC Hydra is set apart as secret phrase wafer. It is amazingly well known secret word saltine and comprises of usable and exceptionally experienced improvement group. The Hydra is snappy and stable Network Login Hacking Tool. It underpins various system conventions including however not limited to AFP, Cisco, AAA, Cisco auth, Cisco empower, CVS, Firebird and so on.

8. Aircrack-ng

Aircrack-ng is ordered among Wi-Fi hacking tools. These devices are renowned in light of the fact that they are successful when utilized properly. Those people who are new to Wireless Specific Hacking program, it is suggested for them. It's hacking devices can recuperate keys when adequate information packets have been secured in screen mode.

9. John the Ripper

John the Ripper is the mainstream secret key splitting pen testing tools that is especially used to execute lexicon assaults. John the Ripper has been granted for having a decent name. It is regularly alluded as "John". This device can likewise be utilized to complete various adjustments to lexicon assaults.

10. Putty

Putty isn't a hacking device, yet it is an exceptionally advantageous tool for a programmer. It fills in as a customer for SSH and Telnet, which can associate PCs remotely. It is additionally used to convey SSH burrowing to sidestep firewalls. Along these lines, this was about the best hacking devices utilized by programmers and pen analyzers for hacking reason.

CHAPTER SIX

Foot Printing

Foot Printing

What is the initial step one would take before looking for confirmation in a college or school? Unanimously, it must be essential research about the establishment. Footprinting is a closely resembling venture which programmers take before obtaining entrance into any system. The precise footprinting of an association empowers assailants to make a total profile of an association's security stance like framework design, arrange squares and IP tends to uncovered on the Internet. Programmers gain surveillance of the objective after a succession of steps as:

Open Source Foot printing-The initial step a programmer takes is to visit the site of a potential objective. He at that point searches for contact data of the chairmen which may help in speculating the secret key or in Social Engineering.

System Enumeration-This is the following stage in picking up data where the programmer attempts to distinguish the area names and the system squares of the objective system.

Checking once the system square is known, the following stage is to spy for dynamic IP addresses on the objective system The Internet Control Message Protocol (ICMP) is a decent option for distinguishing dynamic IP addresses.

Individuals Searching

There are a large number of or billions of ventures directed once a day on all mainstream web crawlers just as the well known interpersonal interaction stages. Anyway what precisely these men look for involves our worry. There are a few stages or devices that can be utilized to figure out what precisely individuals look for on these web search tools.

5 Steps People Use to Search Pipl

What you will discover when you visit Pipl is that this internet searcher doesn't simply look through the web, yet rather experiences looking through a region this website alludes to as the Invisible web. There are some shrouded assets on the Internet that web crawlers essentially can't or don't access for an assortment of reasons. Some contain individual data, and the destinations containing that data quit being filed by the normal web indexes. Pipl is distinctive in light of the fact that it indexes such data.

What you can include will decide how precise your outcomes might be. In the event that you just have a name, you may get any data on anybody with that name. In the event that you can include progressively, similar to a state, you will get increasingly explicit outcomes.

Wink

Wink looks crosswise over what you would discover utilizing a customary web index just as crosswise over social networks, online profiles, and so forth. A few people scans work by searching for however many conceivable outcomes as could be allowed, yet Wink works in a practically inverse way. Wink looks for known data, so any propelled terms you enter should be certainties, similar to a birthday or city of birth about which you are sure. Potential outcomes will just confound and constrain unreasonably your outcomes. Hence, Wink is especially helpful for the individuals who know a ton of fundamental individual data about the individual they are attempting to discover.

Facebook

Facebook is one of the world's biggest interpersonal organizations with a huge number of individuals on this stage every day, it bodes well to utilize Facebook as an unbelievably valuable apparatus to discover individuals on the web. This stage is utilized by billions of individuals over the world yet just a couple of individuals realize how to appropriately utilize this site. Facebook is regularly a broadly utilized internet systems administration program that enables people groups to impart data to other individuals. You can even keep an eye on people groups, discover people groups filling in as an Artist, Singer, Professionals, and so forth., and reach them for your motivation.

PeekYou

PeekYou is a fascinating turn to the world, it enables you to scan for usernames over an assortment of social networking. PeekYou believes itself to be "The Smartest People Search Online." It is a site that brings individuals from everywhere throughout the world together. Anybody with a Peek You profile enables other individuals to find their sites, photographs, person to person communication pages, or some other contact data they have given on the web.

LinkedIn

LinkedIn is totally free however they do have an ace rendition which gives you much more highlights, for example, the master record shows what watchwords raise your profile, what industry these individuals are in when they have seen your profile, and where they are found geologically. You can likewise observe everybody who has ever looked at your profile while the free form just demonstrates to you the five latest. By and large, in case you're simply beginning, the free form is all you need. LinkedIn can be a goldmine for you in the event that you realize how to target people groups and sell your stuff or take get a new line of work with LinkedIn

Virtual box For Hacking

A large number of you have been experiencing issues setting up your hacking condition to rehearse your hacks. In this part, I will demonstrate to you the most straightforward and quickest approach to set up a lab to rehearse your hacks before taking them out into this present reality where any slip-ups could be destroying.

Download VMware Workstation or Box

The most ideal approach to work on hacking is inside a virtual situation. Basically, you set up a hacking framework, for example, Kali Linux, and a few unfortunate casualties to abuse in a perfect world, you would need various working frameworks (Windows XP, Vista, 7, and 8, as well as a Linux/Unix) and applications so you can evaluate an assortment of hacks.

Virtual machines and a virtual system are the best and most secure approach to set up a hacking lab. There are a few virtualization frameworks out there, including Citrix, Oracle's Virtual Box, KVM, Microsoft's Virtual PC and Hyper-V, and VMware's Workstation, VMware Box. For a research center condition, I firmly prescribe VMware's Workstation or Box.

Download Kali VMware Images

When you have downloaded and introduced your virtualization framework, our subsequent stage is to download the VMware pictures of Kali given by Offensive Security, you won't need to make the virtual machine, however essentially run it from Workstation or Box — This implies once you have downloaded the VM of Kali, you would then be able to utilize it in either Workstation or Box without really introducing another OS

Open Image with VMware

When every one of the records has been unfastened, our subsequent stage is to open this new virtual machine. Cause note of the area where you to have unfastened the virtual machine picture. At that point, go to either VMware Workstation or Box and go to File > Create new Machine > Allocate Ram and HDD Space > Select ISO File and Install the new OS in VMware

Download & Install Targets

For the following stage, you have to download and introduce an objective framework. Obviously, you could utilize your host Windows 7 or 8 framework, yet since this is practice, you should utilize a more established, simpler to hack framework. Likewise, hacking your framework can leave it shaky and harmed.

I suggest introducing a Windows XP, Vista, Server 2003, or a more established variant of Linux. These frameworks have many realized security defects that you can rehearse on and, at that point when you become increasingly capable at hacking, and you would then be able to move up to Windows 7 and 8 and more current variants of Linux.

On the off chance that you or your companions don't have a duplicate of these more established working frameworks, you can buy them economically numerous spots on the Internet. Obviously, you can likewise acquire these working frameworks for nothing on a large number of the deluge destinations, however, BEWARE... you will probably be downloading something beyond the working frameworks. Regularly, these free downloads incorporate rootkits that will insert in your framework when you open the record.

Download Old Applications

When you have your working framework set up, frequently you will require applications to keep running on these more established adaptations of the Windows and Linux working frameworks. You will probably require a program, Office, Adobe items, and so on. These more seasoned items have surely understood security defects that you can sharpen your aptitudes on.

Reconnaissance:

In the PC world, there are heroes who make organizes that help us discuss, work with others and get data and after that, there are those not all that great folks who, for an assortment of reasons, as to utilize their PCs to worm their way into those systems and cause inconvenience.

They're called hackers, and they'll routinely do things like:

- Steal secrets.
- Obtain passwords.
- Get credit card information.
- Create so much traffic that a site needs to close down.

Programmers are ALWAYS at work, either attempting to take data for their very own addition or upset nothing new. You hear a great deal of about programmers on the news from time to time, however exactly what's going on with them?

Here's a touch of foundation to enable you to comprehend what it implies when a site or organization is "hacked." Programmers aren't saints.

For reasons unknown, there are the individuals who believe that programmers are "cool" and that their soul of naughtiness and sneaking is honorable. Yet, the IT (Information innovation) specialists who spend a great deal of cash building business or government systems would oppose this idea. Also, so far as that is concerned, so would any individual who has ever had their cash or character taken by a programmer. There's nothing fun-loving about that.

A great many people would concur that there are **three sorts of programmers:**

- **Young kids**"having a fabulous time." These are youths who are basically vandals on the Internet and are otherwise called Script Kiddies. They're not searching for over a couple of hours of their fun disturbing sites or systems.
- **Recreational "programmers."**These are adroit PC clients who meddle with systems when they believe they have a legitimate explanation to...in their brains, in any event, they may have resentment against a specific site or organization and take their abhorrence out by "hacking" or disturbing the site.
- **Professionals**. At the point when a PC master experiences hacking and prefers the flavor, the individual will keep on utilizing their ability, regularly for breaking into individuals' records to take cash. They likewise may like bringing down a major system "for no particular reason."

Stealing passwords and getting in the system.

Discovering a secret key is typically the initial phase in splitting a system's security. (That is the reason there are such a large number of articles guiding you to change your passwords regularly and make them difficult to make sense of!)

Here are a couple of key terms that you'll hear in discourses about programmers and what they do:

Buffer overflow:A technique for assault where the programmer conveys malignant directions to a framework by overwhelming an application cushion.

Denial of service attack: An assault intended to disable the injured individual's framework by keeping it from taking care of its typical traffic, for the most part by flooding it with false traffic.

Email worm: An infection loaded content or smaller than usual program sent to a clueless unfortunate casualty through an ordinary-looking email message.

Root access: The most significant level of access (and most wanted by genuine programmers) to a PC framework, which can give them full oversight over the framework.

Rootkit:A lot of apparatuses utilized by an interloper to extend and camouflage his control of the framework.

Script kiddie: A youthful or unsophisticated programmer who uses base programmer devices to attempt to act as a genuine programmer.

Session hijacking: At the point when a programmer can embed malevolent information bundles directly into a genuine information transmission over the Internet association.

Trojan horse: An apparently supportive program that fools the PC client into opening it, just to convey (unnoticed and in the background) a sudden assault on the client's PC.

CHAPTER SEVEN

Using VPN & TOR

Using VPN AND TOR

Utilizing an intermediary server isn't totally verify, however. To speak with your ideal server giving the site you need to visit, the intermediary needs to decode your traffic and in this manner the internet service of the intermediary server can see the decoded information stream. This can be maintained a strategic distance from by fastening intermediaries together or by essentially utilizing an assistance like Tor which diverts your traffic through three intermediaries, supposed "hubs." This way, it is practically difficult to distinguish you, yet...

The 'enormous however' here is, that the leave hub unscrambles your traffic again to speak with the server you are attempting to reach, for example Google.com. This implies the leave hub can undoubtedly keep an eye on the substance of the bundles you send through the tor organize, as for example decoded passwords and everything else which isn't SSL scrambled. This can be utilized against you from numerous points of view:

Totally everybody may give a Tor hub. The administration, offenders ... Despite the fact that the leave hub suppliers don't have a clue who is sending and mentioning the traffic being diverted through their hub, they can utilize the information they can "phish" thusly against you at any rate. Besides, it is entirely simple to make sense of who you are by essentially translating the recorded bundles.

An option in contrast to Tor and comparable administrations are VPN administrations. Same issue applies here: The VPN specialist co-op can undoubtedly see your decoded traffic and use it against you. It occurred in any event once that law requirement penetrated such an assistance and brought an entire association of web crooks down.

The end therefor is that such approaches to stay mysterious may be proficient yet you are constantly compelled to confide in the supplier of the intermediary/VPN administration you need to utilize. In all actuality, this can't be accomplished. You don't have the foggiest idea who is behind a help and regardless of whether this individual can be believed, the person in question won't be permitted to disclose to you that the administration is penetrated by the legislature, also the threat of such administrations being hacked.

Tips for Using VPN And Tor online (www.torproject.org).A VPN or a virtual private system broadens a specific private system over the open system and this incorporates the web. It empowers the clients to send just as get the information over the open systems and the common systems. This is done as though they are registering gadgets and these gadgets are associated with the private system. A VPN is made by setting up a point to point association by utilizing different committed associations, traffic encryption and burrowing conventions. This is essentially particularly like the WAN that can likewise be called as a wide region organize. You ought to pursue these underneath tips to be a certain client of a VPN.

•Your firewall ought to be up and be running

This can sound somewhat troublesome and minor. Anyway a firewall ought to be on and running inevitably and it doesn't make a difference whether you are utilizing a VPN or not, the firewall must be ready for action 24 hours per day.

•You must remain undercover i.e. use incognito mode

Numerous individuals nowadays consistently overlook that their program can give away an immense measure of individual data. This generally happens when the client isn't utilizing an in secret or a protected mode while utilizing the site. There are likewise a few sites that advise the client to go in disguise when it isn't verify and you as a client must need to do it.

•Disable all the geo-area administrations

A large number of us are utilizing cell phones and tablets for ordinary utilize like Facebook and YouTube. Each one of the individuals who basically need to utilize every one of these gadgets need to watch out for all the geo-area administrations and

•Manage all your cookies

Nowadays nobody in their bustling life gives any consideration to cookies. Anyway these cookies are all over the place and this treats regularly attempt to improve the intermittent perusing of the web. These cookies be changed and altered into different following contents and these can screen your movement just as the system data.

•The VPN over a TOR

TOR is presumably an exceptionally major ordeal when this specific innovation had turned out and furthermore a group of us have utilized this TOR program to utilize the Facebook at work. You can likewise depend on the TOR yourself. It is an exceptionally extraordinary and furthermore an open source arrangement that is accessible for every one of the stages. It is one of the significant things to recall.

A VPN (Virtual Private Network) interfaces a PC or PC over the Internet to the workplace system enabling the remote client to fill in as though they were sitting at their work area in the workplace. Ordinarily, setting up a VPN requires noteworthy specialized aptitudes as the workplace firewall should be reconfigured, the VPN server must be arrangement and the entire part must be made secure. When arrangement and working, the VPN server should be checked (to guarantee there is nothing suspicious going on) and kept up with the most recent security patches given by the VPN seller.

Be that as it may, there is an elective method to arrangement a VPN by utilizing a VPN administration. A VPN administration gives every one of the highlights of a VPN server however expels the intricacy and cost of arrangement, observing and upkeep. To arrangement a VPN gave as an assistance, you have to visit the supplier's site, register on the web and download a bit of programming to a framework in the workplace organize. This product associates the workplace system to the VPN Service by means of the Internet without changing your firewall. By not changing your firewall, you have expelled a potential assault point for programmers who output firewalls to recognize shortcomings. When the workplace system is associated, you would then be able to add clients to the administration and arrangement their PCs for VPN get to. The further developed VPN administrations give an approach to give the remote client a chance to set themselves up for access to the workplace so that close to enlisting, a remote client can be taking a shot at their applications and documents as though they were in the workplace.

Some facilitated VPN benefits just give access to an individual's very own PC which implies that their office PC should consistently be fueled on and that they have a PC/Laptop when out of the workplace. While these sort of VPN administrations work, they are not very eco-accommodating (you need a fueled on PC for every remote client) and they don't bolster exercises, for example, making and perusing mail when there is no web get to

Other VPN administrations associate the remote client to the workplace organize as though their PC was on an exceptionally long link. With these administrations a remote client associates straightforwardly to the document and mail servers without utilizing a work area PC. With this sort of access, individuals utilize their workstation the very same path all through the workplace without recollecting whether a record was put away on a server or on the PC. Mail applications, for example, Microsoft Outlook work particularly well on a system VPN as they enable the client to peruse and make mail notwithstanding when they are not associated with the VPN. At the point when the client next associates with the VPN, standpoint will consequently send all the recently made mail. Some VPN administrations will likewise give a safe method to access mail and records from any internet browser so remote clients don't have to have a workstation with them consistently.

Recommended VPN Providers

www.hidemvass.com

www.ipvanish.com

www.expressvpn.com

www.cvberghost.com

www.hsselite.com

Setting up VPN

Setting up a VPN should be possible for different purposes, for example, for Remote Access over the Internet, Connecting Networks over the Internet and Connecting Computers over an Intranet. The point of VPN is to give indistinguishable administrations from that got through costly rented lines, yet at a lower cost.

Here is a gander at the progression engaged with setting up a VPN in your home PC. Select 'Control Panel' from the 'Start' menu. Here you have to choose "System and Internet Settings" and from here select 'System Connections' in XP or the Network and Sharing Center in Vista. Continue to finish the means here by choosing 'Make a New Connection'. Next pursue the up and coming strides till you complete the 'Permit Virtual Private Connections' progression. Select the check box for every client that you need to give access over the VPN. This procedure finishes the VPN arrangement. You can see new approaching associations now.

You have to visit a VPN specialist co-op's site. Register online in the website and download the product to any framework in the workplace organize. This downloaded programming builds up association between the workplace systems with the VPN administration through the web with no compelling reason to change in the firewall. By leaving the firewall unaltered, the system is profoundly verified from the programmers. You can add clients to the administration once the workplace system is associated. The clients can arrangement their PCs for VPN get to. There are progressed VPN administration accessible, which enables the remote client to work following enrollment.

VPN administration helps in constrained equipment obtainment and utilizing advisors to arrangement in this manner giving opportunity to include or expel clients at proprietor's prerequisite.

Change or Spoof a Mac Address in Windows

Each Network Interface Card has an uncommon MAC address. This applies to a wide scope of framework cards, including Ethernet cards and Wi-Fi cards. The MAC Address is a six-byte number or 12-digit hexadecimal number that is used to surprisingly recognize a host on a framework

Various Ways of Finding Your MAC Address:

There are a few different ways of finding your Ethernet and correspondences convention data. Numerous Ethernet card producers have restrictive programming that can uncover this data, however they work diversely relying upon the maker. So we will utilize the Windows 2000 and XP "ipconfig" utility since this is accessible in most of Windows Operating Systems.

To start with, go to "start" - > "run" and type "cmd" without the quotation. At that point hit the enter key. At the order line type "ipconfig/all", again without the statements. All things considered, simply composing ipconfig without the/all will work yet will just give you truncated data in regards to your system cards. A case of what you may see by composing the "ipconfig/all" direction is beneath:

Yield of the "Ipconfig/All" Command

Recommended Tool for changing Mac Address

MacMakeUp- https://macmakeup.en.softonic.com/

MacMakeUp permits to changing MAC address to one of your decision or randomized one. Since initial couple of images of MAC are code for equipment producer application additionally has the inner rundown of those codes you can browse.

There are some exceptional settings, yet I recommend they are not to be tinkered with except if you have valid justification to. Same similarly as with real MAC address altering

CHAPTER EIGHT

Social Engineering

Social Engineering

Kids' appear as though they see how to apply the Concept of social designing. Kids makes bunches of clamor with guarantee of being calm just when they get the toy or outing they need. Individuals are likewise controlled mentally until they do what programmers needs, for example, surrender individual or private data on the web and disconnected. Like DDoS (appropriated refusal of administration) is generally one of numerous parts of a plan with objectives of blackmail, framework or system get to, gift, harassing, data fraud, business demolition, human and medication dealing, and different sorts of misrepresentation and criminal behavior. On the other side, these social designing and hacking blend of exercises may have an objective of "helping an apparent social imbalance" or accomplishing logical research.

Some state that Kevin Mitnick, when known as the world's most needed programmer, is the person who previously begat the expression "social designing." The expression has an awful notoriety on the web, yet whether it is a positive or negative action is as a top priority of the spectator similarly as DDoS, telephone tricks, and different exercises that may social building assault on the web and disconnected. Each time a lady or a man does anything in the endeavor to get others to do what she or he needs, that is social designing.

Once more, social designing is the demonstration of hoodwinking a person into uncovering data that ought to be private or into accomplishing something the individual in question would not ordinarily do. The casualties of such are not really simple or insensible. Possibly it is only that they trust essentially everybody. They appreciate helping other people. Then again, the culprits of social building are speaking to all inclusive, time-safe human wants and feelings: desire, companionship, influence, karma, cash, avarice, retribution, philanthropy, achievement, popularity, and being a piece of a greater reason. Culprits can without much of a stretch stunt individuals into surrendering data that they have no clue is bound to bargain a server, PC, business, family, arrange, or other on the web or disconnected individual, place, thing, thought or association.

Hacking is the demonstration of entering a PC framework by means of a security break; though, social building is as an attack of the psyche. Have you known about passionate knowledge? Individuals with sharp passionate insight cause extraordinary social designers and can make unimaginable things to happen similarly as PC framework programmers can. Join the two and find conceivably relentless coordinated efforts that can unleash agonizing destruction, crazy virtuoso, mind blowing change-production or enormous achievement for associations and people on the web and disconnected. Sounds terrible, isn't that right? Be that as it may, the two are consolidated from the beginning of time for good and malevolence, contingent on your perspective.

Social Engineering Expert: Hacker's Greatest Tool

It is the craft of controlling individuals into accomplishing something, such as unveiling secret data or performing activities that would uncover data, and making them like doing it, I.e. they "illuminated" an issue or helped somebody, and so forth. This enables the programmer to acquire data in a non-undermining way. Give us now a chance to investigate a few models how simple it is for a programmer to use social building to get private or delicate data.

There are a few models where social building can be utilized for individual increase, other than unveiling data. One regular model that is utilized by numerous individuals consistently: paying a compliment to the lady at a fine eatery figuring you might be situated at a more pleasant table or situated quicker, or doing likewise to your server or server to get quicker help.

Very regularly in the present society, social designing is being utilized for questionable reasons, so a programmer can get delicate individual and additionally organization data. This has now turned into a genuine risk to the security of your representatives, secret customer data, and friends records or potentially banking data.

Here are a portion of the social designing stunts and tricks:

• The IT Support Person Scam:

The social specialist accesses your PC frameworks by calling as an IT bolster individual. By and large, this is simpler to do when there is a great deal of buzz about infection or malware in the media. It can, in any case, occur whenever. The individual acting like IT support (the sham) considers a client and endeavors to lead them through some kind of fix for the malware. The fraud keeps on focusing on how significant fixing this is and makes the end client become disappointed. When the client winds up baffled, the fraud says something along the individual picking up the telephone has neglected to report for jury obligation, or show up as required by a subpoena. This generally overwhelms the answerer. The guest at that point requests the answerer's complete name, government managed savings number, and date of birth, so they may "confirm" they are the individual who neglected to show up. The clueless promptly supplies this data

- Disaster Relief Scam:

This trick as a rule happens directly after a fiasco, for example, a typhoon or has happened most as of late the besieging at the Boston Marathon. Counterfeit gift locales show up on the web by the hundreds or even thousands. The reason oi these locales is to utilize the enthusiastic intrigue of helping exploited people to catch Visa or financial balance data from the individuals who are benevolent, and might want to help. We certainly urge the individuals who wish to help in these circumstances, BUT, look at the site and the establishment set up before you give.

- Unconditional Present cards or Airline Tickets:

This sort of danger happens regularly by means of email on Facebook, Tumblr, and Pinterest. The client is incited with an "advertisement" that shows that the client will get an unconditional present card or programming redesign or maybe even some of Bill Gates fortune, for filling in a review. Remain away!!! These organizations are not so much giving endlessly anything. They are only gathering data from the clueless that can be utilized to take an Identity.

• Unapproved Access to Your Building or Offices:

Ordinarily somebody will hang out in a smoking territory and visiting it up with individual smokers who approach a safe structure or office. At the point when the genuine representatives go to enter the office, the sham just tails them utilizing a method called "closely following." If the workers approach the fraud for their ID, get to card, or identification, the faker will essentially tell the representatives they left their entrance card in their office. "Cigarettes, a Social Engineer's closest companion."

Another method for increasing unapproved access to your structure or workplaces is for the "fraud" to have heaps of bundles or essentially state "I'm in a rush, if you don't mind let me in".

Social Engineering is setting down deep roots. In the event that it sounds unrealistic or workers feel something simply doesn't feel right, they should confide in their gut nature. Chances are except if you are cautious, you won't realize you are an unfortunate casualty until it is past the point of no return. It is imperative to have an expressed IT strategy set up, just as a wellbeing approach, and to have your workers acquainted with them two. The more mindful they can be I hide likely you, your representatives, or your organization will Irtoiiu* the* injured individual or a reluctant programmer.

Ways To Use Public Wi-Fi to hack Identity

1. Man-in-the-Middle Attacks

The mechanical term, man-in-the-middle (MITM) : an assault whereby an outsider captures interchanges between two members. Rather than information being shared legitimately among server and customer, that connection Is broken by another component. The excluded robber at that point shows their very own adaptation of a site to show to you, including their own messages.

Anybody utilizing open Wi-Fi is particularly helpless against a MITM assault. Since the data transmitted is for the most part decoded, it's not simply the hotspot that is open it's your information as well. You should yell out your subtleties, A traded off switch can vacuum up a great deal of individual material moderately essentially: simply getting into your messages, for example, gives programmers access to your usernames, passwords, and private messages.

2. Counterfeit Wi-Fi Connections

This variety of a MITM assault is otherwise called the "Insidious Twin". The strategy catches your information in travel, yet sidesteps any security frameworks an open Wi-Fi hotspot may have. The issue brought about by interfacing with a vindictive switch. All things considered, clients were coordinated into an outsider FIR Intelligence as a matter of fact improbable, yet truly, exploited people could be giving over the entirety of their private data, simply in light of the fact that they were fooled into joining an inappropriate system.

It's genuinely simple to set up a phony passageway (AP), and is definitely justified even despite the exertion for cybercriminals. They can utilize any gadget with web abilities, including a cell phone, to set up an AP with a similar name as a real hotspot. Any transmitted information sent subsequent to joining a phony system goes by means of a programmer.

3. Bundle Sniffing

It's a diverting name, yet the real routine with regards to "packet sniffing" is a long way from a snickering matter. This technique empowers a programmer to get airborne data at that point break down it at their own speed. A gadget transmits an information packet over a decoded system, which would then be able to be perused by free programming like Wireshark. Truth is stranger than fiction: it's free. Look on the web and you'll even observe "how to" guides, showing you how to utilize Wireshark. Why? Since it's a convenient device for investigating web traffic, including, incidentally enough, discovering cybercriminals and vulnerabilities that need fixing.

4. Session Hijacking

Side jacking depends on acquiring data by means of bundle sniffing. Rather than utilizing that information retroactively, nonetheless, a programmer utilizes it on-area. Surprisingly more terrible, it sidesteps a few degrees of encryption! Sign in subtleties are commonly sent through a scrambled system (ideally) and checked utilizing the record data held by the site. This at that point reacts utilizing treats sent to your gadget. Cabin the last isn't constantly scrambled — a programmer can commandeer your session and can access any private records you're signed into,

5. Shoulder-Surfing

At whatever point utilizing an ATM, you should check everyone around you, ensuring nobody's looking as you enter your PIN. It's likewise a threat with regards to open Wi-Fi. It at least one people are drifting around when you're visiting private destinations, remain suspicious. Try not to submit anything individual like a secret key. It's an essential trick, however one that absolutely still works tor tricksters and programmers.

CHAPTER NINE

Hackers, Hoaxes and Spyware

Everybody who has an ISP, comprehends, or if nothing else thinks about how programmers use infections, Trojans, and other web nasties, to contaminate and wreckage up your PC. No feature news there. (Shockingly, despite everything we don't comprehend why they do it, or if nothing else I don't.] But programmers don't need to compose noxious code or seize your program to do some genuine harm to your framework. God help us... An elegantly composed email without any connections can work. They just need to begin gossip.

Programmers can undoubtedly control you into destroying your own PC. They should simply start a lie.

Scams work fantastically well for getting normal individuals to make their very own PCs glitch. The programmer doesn't need to invest any energy making malevolent code and a strategy for conveyance, they should simply play on the human propensity for insanity; convey a notice that something fiendishness is spreading, and in the event that you discover it on your PC, dispose of it! As of late I was following a string on a discussion, where the mediator cautioned everybody about a document that he found on his framework that was a key lumberjack. (A key lumberjack is a malignant program intended to follow everything you might do through observing your keystrokes.) He cautioned everybody to scan for a record, ans2000.ini and, "erase the booger."

Deceptions are similarly as hazardous as live infections, since they motivate you to obliterate your very own projects. I am certain they are a specific kick for the one beginning the trick, as they are getting you to do terrible things to your very own framework. Dread is an incredible spark, and fabrications, by configuration, are made to cause frenzy and dread in the less experienced Internet explorer.

Along these lines, before proceeding to erase records from your hard drive, go look at them. Do a quest for them and read the data you find. Don't simply go erasing things without finding out about them first, or you just may wind up cutting your own throat. Also, NEVER forward these kinds of caution messages to others until you know beyond all doubt that the data is right, or you're probably going to have your loved ones after you for misleading them.

Eliminating Spyware, Adwares, and Viruses

Preventing Malicious Processes from Getting Installed:

Do not download all kinds of random stuff!

For instance, it's OK to download an image (by right clicking it and picking "Spare Picture As") from a site. There is no mischief in this, for the most part. In any case, downloading screensavers and "free" games and other apparently free programming continually isn't great. It doesn't mean all free stuff is terrible, simply be cautious just to download free projects from destinations you trust (huge name locales are frequently a decent decision).

It's additionally OK to open a connection from a companion you trust, yet abstain from opening and perusing email advances, particularly in the event that they have connections! Email advances start with "FW:"- ask companions who send advances not to send them, as you don't open or peruse them in any case. Advances are ostensibly an exercise in futility and ones with connections are not worth the hazard.

When you download and introduce a program, don't simply click Next or Yes when the establishment prompts you with choices. Uncheck boxes with toolbars and other additional items that you may not need.

Don't simply introduce things when incited while surfing the net!

At the point when, a site says, "This site needs to introduce bla," ensure it's a site you trust and that you REALLY NEED whatever you are attempting to get to. For instance, on the off chance that you are on a noteworthy telecom organization's site attempting to watch a video, it's clearly alright, If you are on some obscure site attempting to get something, reconsider.

In the event that you weren't attempting to get anything by any stretch of the imagination, certainly click the red X in the corner! Never click Yes or No, simply click the Red X. In the event that that doesn't work, press ALT+F4 on your console to close the site!

Eliminating Things Manually

Stop unneeded processes!

Press CTRL+ALT+DEL (all at once] and see what is running in the Processes tab. See something you don't recognize? Google it. On the off chance that it's not required, you'll need to end it by right clicking it and picking End Process. Do this whenever your framework misbehaves. Experience the rundown and check whether anything bizarre is there, at that point Google it. (NOTE: Don't end something unless you are sure it is not needed!}

Control what runs when Windows starts up!

Click START, go to RUN and type msconfig, then click OK. Choose selective startup and go to the Startup tab. Anything you don't recognize here? Google it. If it's not necessary, uncheck the box. Go through the whole list and do this, then click OK and restart when you are ready. After rebooting, Windows will remind you that you've chosen selective startup.

CHAPTER TEN

Malware

Malware

Malware is a frequently utilized, yet only from time to time comprehended term that is utilized to by and large portray vindictive projects that character cheats, programmers and Internet extortionists use to control your PC and use it to perform assignments with you as the client regularly being unaware. Malware incorporates every pernicious program running from irritating adware to the more risky spyware to the staggering effects of PC infections that can open up indirect accesses on your PC, enabling obscure outsiders to control your PC as a major aspect of a zombie armed force to send spam, take personality data and host unlawful substance on the Internet - all under your name and online character.

How Do You Become Infected?

Numerous malware applications are cunningly masked as helpful, even attractive bits of programming that the client botches as real and indiscriminately downloads onto their PC. For instance, if a site offered you the chance to expand the speed of your web for nothing, OK be enticed snap download? Shouldn't something be said about on the off chance that you were offered a preliminary download of the world's '"quickest and most secure" web search tool for nothing?

In an amusing twist on this contamination technique, numerous malware applications are really promoted as hostile to malware devices, and these are not patio tasks — these are proficient looking and exceptionally misleading sites that seem to offer real items.

Malware additionally discovers its direction onto PCs by piggy-support off enormous, real organizations. For instance, Firefox, the world's second most well-known internet browser has truly a large number of supported and homebrew augmentations - some of which may contain malware. Toolbars, errand person augmentations and screensavers are for the most part most loved concealing spots of perilous malware applications.

Malware is additionally usually introduced onto a framework through Active-X controls: uncommon projects that can change your PC's library and truly assume responsibility for specific PC capacities. While Active-X controls can be perilous, they are likewise utilized authentically for a wide range of employments. Time after time clients wind up contaminated with malware just by being excessively trusting and clicking 'Acknowledge' just too rapidly.

Malware can be propelled from practically any web connection, picture or video, implying that person to person communication destinations like Facebook and Google+ are strict reproducing justification for malware applications as recordings and pictures 'circulate around the web', contaminating immense quantities of connected PCs rapidly.

What Does Malware Do?

As referenced previously, the elements of malware extend from irritating to crushing. The absolute most regular capacities off malware include:

The accumulation and transmission of individual subtleties, account data and passwords back to an obscure outsider server, Serving the client with undesirable and tireless publicizing, If a client enters an off base web address, the program can divert them to a business or trading off site, The client's landing page can be seized and changed to a business or phishing site, Changing a web-program's security settings and working capacity, making it simpler for security to be undermined, decreasing the general execution of the client's PC... before diverting them to a library cleaning item or framework enhancer.

Malware and spyware are unquestionably genuine dangers for anybody utilizing a PC that is associated with the Internet. Malware is any program with a motivation behind penetrating a PC without client learning of the contamination with the reason to harm the framework, take data, or simply be irritating to the client. Spyware is a particular kind of malware which is portrayed by the plan to take individual data from a client. PC clients need to attack with regards to keeping their frameworks clean from diseases while surfing the Internet. A mix of keeping the most recent fix levels on the two Windows refreshes just as infection filter mark refreshes related to being cautious with regards to the kinds of destinations a client visits and makes themselves accessible to will enormously lessen the chances of disease.

Malware can be a huge risk to Internet clients. Malware programming presents itself in various manners and by and large, it harms a PC to the point where a client essentially needs to reload the working framework. The outcomes can be:

Corrupted records

• Stolen individual data including Visa numbers, financial balances, and so on.

• Annoying spring up promotions that a client expel

There are five kinds of malware out there today

(1) Contagious Software: This kind of programming is made out of PC infections or alleged worms. This kind of malware is the most well-known. An "infection" depicts a PC infection instead of a genuine physical infection which may taint us. Infections are unique in relation to worms in their circulation and the real activity.

The main kind of malware to develop was the PC infection. Infections work and spread inside the tainted framework by joining themselves to other programming. On account of large scale infections, to reports. During the execution of the program, the viral code is executed. Infections spread crosswise over PCs when the product or archive they appended themselves to is moved from PC to PC.

The PC worm, used to contaminate frameworks, started when the web was first utilized. The worm checks various systems in the PC, testing for any helpless frameworks where it can duplicate itself. From this new base, inside your PC the worm starts filtering and duplicating itself to every single powerless record or procedures. Despite the fact that worms and infections had unmistakable implications and utilizations, they currently are utilized to show any kind of infectious malware.

PC worms are remain solitary programming and therefore don't require different bits of programming to join themselves to. They are begun as a feature of the boot procedure. Worms spread, either by abusing some defenselessness of the objective framework, or by utilizing some sort of social building to fool clients into executing them.

(2) Hidden documents: This kind of malware is utilized to shroud any sort of movement inside a client's PC. There are different sorts of concealed records, for example, (an) A Trojan. These are the commonplace Trojan ponies. They fill a similar need as the legendary Trojan pony. You know, the one the Greeks used to assume control over Troy. A few Trojans are enrolled on your PC as utilities. At the point when the client downloads the malware, an entryway opens for different sorts of malware to be brought into the framework.

Trojan steeds are get executed by being a piece of a generally helpful bit of programming. Trojan steeds are connected to the host programming physically, they can't contaminate different bits of programming the way infections can, nor would they be able to reproduce themselves. Trojan steeds depend on the helpful highlights of the host programming, which stunt clients to introduce them. One of the most guileful sorts of Trojan steed is a program that cases PC episode of the infection. By bringing the infection into one system by means of a Trojan steed, the maker sees the spread of the infection to different systems.

(3) A Backdoor: A Backdoor is a bit of programming that enables access to the PC framework, bypassing the typical confirmation methods. This infection makes an elective entryway inside your structure. It makes an alternate pathway or course to the treats. This infection evades any security framework dwelling on your PC. Once inside the framework through the secondary passage, the programmer will have the option to would anything they like to do.

There are two gatherings of indirect accesses. The main gathering works much like a Trojan. They are physically embedded into another bit of programming, executed by means of their host programming and

(4) An Exploit: A bit of programming that assaults a specific security helplessness. Endeavors are not really noxious in expectation - they are regularly concocted by security scientists as a method for exhibiting that a weakness exists. Be that as it may, they are a typical part of malignant projects, for example, organize worms.

(5) Phony or Hoax Viruses: There are cases where trick infection cautioning messages have been sent which recommend that the beneficiary may have a specific infection, together with supportive directions about how to affirm and dispose of the infection. These messages constantly instruct you to search for a specific record and in the event that it is available, erase it. Much of the time, the record which they notice is a Windows framework document which whenever erased will cause genuine running issues.

CHAPTER ELEVEN

SQL (Structured Query Language)

SQL (Structured Query Language)

SQL represents Structured Query Language and is a decisive programming language used to get to and control information in RDBMS (Relational Database Management Systems). SQL was created by IBM in 70's for their centralized computer stage. Quite a long while later SQL wound up institutionalized by both American National Standards Institute (ANSI-SQL) and International Organization for Standardization (ISO-SQL). As indicated by ANSI SQL is articulated "es line el", yet numerous product and database engineers with foundation in MS SQL Server articulate it "continuation".

SQL is overwhelmingly utilized by 2 kinds of clients - projects and people (entering in the directions through a database customer) - to pass guidelines to databases. SQL directions can be entered into a database customer like the MySQL Query Browser or the SQL Server Enterprise Manager and executed to either restore an outcome or alter records in the database. SQL can likewise be utilized related to a programming language or scripting dialects like Microsoft Visual Basic or PHP to speak with the database.

In spite of the fact that SQL is a world standard, tragically most database sellers have concocted various lingos and varieties.

This is on the grounds that each database seller needs to separate its database items from the group. One genuine model is Microsoft SQL server's TRANSACT-SQL. Execute SQL is a superset of SQL and is intended for utilizing just with Microsoft SQL Server. In spite of the fact that it makes programming a lot simpler for programming designers, it isn't consistent with different databases like Oracle or MySQL - making TRANSACT-SQL programs non-database-convenient. Such, albeit a considerable lot of these highlights are amazing and hearty, it is great practice to exercise alert and confines your SQL use to be consistent with the ANSI/ISO SQL principles and ODBC-Compliant.

What is RDBMS?

A Relational Database Management System is a bit of programming used to store and oversee information in database articles called tables. A social database table is a forbidden information structure orchestrated in segments and lines. The table sections otherwise called table fields have one of a kind names and various qualities characterizing the segment type, default esteem, lists, and a few other segment attributes. The columns of the social database table are the real information passages.

SQL Injection is one of the many web assault tools utilized by programmers to take information from associations. It is maybe one of the most widely recognized application layer assault procedures utilized today.

Web applications permit real site guests to submit and recover information to/from a database over the web utilizing their favored internet browser.

Databases are fundamental to present day sites - they store information required for sites to convey explicit substance to guests and render data to client's providers, representatives and a large group of partners. Client accreditations, money related and installment data, organization insights may all be inhabitant inside a database and gotten to by authentic clients through off-the-rack and custom web applications. Web applications and databases enable you to normally maintain your business.

SQL Injection is the hacking procedure which endeavors to go SQL directions through a web application for execution by the backend database. If not cleaned appropriately, web applications may result in SQL Injection assaults that enable programmers to see data from the database as well as even wipe it out.

Such highlights as login pages, backing, and item solicitation structures, input structures, search pages, shopping baskets and the general conveyance of dynamic substance, shape current sites and furnish organizations with the methods important to speak with prospects and clients. These site highlights are largely instances of web applications which might be either obtained off-the-rack or created as bespoke projects.

These site highlights are altogether vulnerable to SQL Injection assaults.

SQL Injection

Take a straightforward login page where an authentic client would enter his username and secret phrase mix to enter a safe territory to see his own subtleties or transfer his remarks in a gathering.

At the point when the authentic client presents his subtleties, SQL Query is produced from these subtleties and submitted to the database for confirmation. In the event that substantial, the client is permitted access, at the end of the day, the web application that controls the login page will speak with the database through a progression of arranged directions in order to confirm the username and secret word blend. On confirmation, the genuine client is allowed fitting access.

Through SQL Injection, the programmer may enter explicitly made SQL directions with the purpose of bypassing the login structure boundary and seeing what lies behind it. This is just conceivable if the sources of info are not appropriately purified (i.e., made resistant) and sent legitimately with the SQL inquiry to the database. SQL Injection vulnerabilities give the way to a programmer to impart legitimately to the database.

The advances powerless against this assault are dynamic content dialects including ASP, ASP.NET, PHP, JSP, and CGI. Every one of the assailants needs to play out a SQL Injection hacking assault is an internet browser, learning of SQL inquiries and innovative mystery to significant table and field names. The sheer straightforwardness of SQL Injection has energized its notoriety.

In SQL Injection, the programmer utilizes SQL questions and imagination to get to the database of delicate corporate information through the web application. '

SQL or Structured Query Language is the programming language that enables you to store, control, and recover information put away in a social database (or an accumulation of tables which compose and structure information). SQL is, truth be told, the main way that a web application (and clients) can connect with the database. Instances of social databases incorporate Oracle, Microsoft Access, MS SQL Server, MySQL, and Filemaker Pro, all of which use SQL as their fundamental structure squares.

SQL directions incorporate SELECT, INSERT, DELETE and DROP TABLE. DROP TABLE is as inauspicious as it sounds and in certainty will dispose of the table with a specific name.

In the genuine situation of the login page model over, the SQL directions got ready for the web application may resemble the accompanying:

SELECT count(*)

FROM users_list_table

WHERE username='FIELD_USERNAME'

AND password='FIELD_PASSWORD"

In plain English, this SQL command (from the web application) instructs the database to match the username and password input by the legitimate user to the combination it has already stored.

Each kind of web application is hardcoded with explicit SQL inquiries that it will execute when playing out its genuine capacities and speaking with the database. On the off chance that any information field of the web application isn't appropriately purified, a programmer may infuse extra SQL directions that widen the scope of SQL directions the web application will execute, in this manner going past the first proposed plan and capacity.

A programmer will subsequently have an unmistakable channel of correspondence (or, in layman terms, a passage) to the database independent of all the interruption recognition frameworks and system security hardware introduced before the physical database server.

Is my database in danger to SQL Injection?

SQL Injection is one of the most widely recognized application layer assaults at present being utilized on the Internet. In spite of the way that it is moderately simple to ensure against SQL Injection, there are countless web applications that stay powerless.

As indicated by the Web Application Security Consortium (WASC) 9% of the all-out hacking occurrences revealed in the media until 27th July 2006 were expected to SQL Injection. Later information from our own exploration demonstrates that about half of the sites we have filtered for the current year are powerless to SQL Injection vulnerabilities.

It might be hard to respond to the inquiry whether your site and web applications are powerless against SQL Injection particularly on the off chance that you are not a software engineer or you are not the individual who has coded your web applications.

Our experience persuades that there is a noteworthy shot that your information is as of now in danger from SQL Injection.

Regardless of whether an assailant can see the information put away on the database or not, generally relies upon how your site is coded to show the aftereffects of the inquiries sent. What is sure is that the aggressor will have the option to execute discretionary SQL Commands on the defenseless framework, either to bargain it or else to acquire data.

On the off chance that inappropriately coded, at that point, you risk having your client and friends information traded off.

What an aggressor accesses additionally relies upon the degree of security set by the database. The database could be set to limit to specific directions as it were. Read access ordinarily is empowered for use by web application back finishes.

Regardless of whether an assailant can't alter the framework, he would even now have the option to peruse significant data.

Effect of SQL Injection

When an assailant understands that a framework is defenseless against SQL Injection, he can infuse SQL Query/Commands through an information structure field. This is equal to giving the assailant your database and enabling him to execute any SQL order including DROP TABLE to the database!

An assailant may execute discretionary SQL explanations on the defenseless framework. This may bargain the honesty of your database and additionally uncover delicate data. Contingent upon the back-end database being used, SQL infusion vulnerabilities lead to changing degrees of information/framework access for the assailant. It might be conceivable to control existing inquiries, to UNION (used to choose related data from two tables] discretionary information, use sub chooses, or add extra questions.

Sometimes, it might be conceivable to peruse in or work out to documents, or to execute shell directions on the hidden working system.

Step by step instructions to Restore SQL Database Easily without Any Difficulty

SQL is application delivered by Microsoft which is utilized extensively for productive information the executives by numerous associations around the globe and has truly turned into a fundamental need of clients everywhere. SQL or the Structured Query Language encourages the clients to inquiry the databases and furthermore to effectively recover data from databases that had been made as of now. In this MS SQL Server, the records are spared in .mdf document position.

With SQL working regularly, information the board is incomparably simple, yet the genuine issue emerges for the clients when any issue comes in this SQL Server. In the event that you are tired of the SQL database defilement pressure which is uncalled-for and furthermore tired of the undesirable obstacle to your work as a result of it, at that point it's about time that you get a SQL Server Restoring Database tool and promptly think - how to reestablish SQL database effectively with no trouble? Just a dependable SQL reestablishing database programming can be the perfect pressure releaser that will remove the information misfortune dread and offer an approach to finish fulfillment.

Why SQL gets corrupted?

Reasons for SQL Server debasement are really the reasons requiring the requirement for SQL recuperation. The debasement is abrupt and can happen suddenly because of a few reasons like:

- The problem in hard drive
- Improper and abnormal framework shutdown incidentally
- Virus or Trojan assault
- Software or equipment breakdown
- Incorrect String to multi-customer database alongside client cancellation of Log document or database in "suspected" mode
- No free plate space accessible while the working of SQL Server
- While MS SQL database is running, plate controllers attempting to access or duplicate the document

These are other such unexpected and unforeseen reasons lead to SQL debasement. It is difficult to turn the time back and keep away from such a thing to occur. Just plausibility with the client is to think How to Restore SQL in the event that he utilizing SQL 2005 and how to reestablish SQL 2000 on the off chance that he is utilizing SQL Server 2000.

Blunders showing up at the hour of debasement

A client can get one of the accompanying blunders at the hour of SQL debasement:

List %ls on %ls in database '%lsr might be degenerate due to articulation assessment changes in this discharge. Drop and re-make the record

- The record *.mdf is missing and needs to reestablish
- Server can't locate the mentioned database table
- Pageld in the page header = (0:0)
- Table Corrupt: Object ID 0, list ID 0, page ID (1:623]
- The procedure couldn't execute 'sp_replcmds' on server
- Internal blunder. Cradle gave to peruse segment worth is excessively little. Run DBCC CHECKDB to check for any defilement
- On changes table that was working, .frm is bolted
- The struggle happened in database 'db_name', table 'table_name', section 'column_name'. The announcement has been ended.

Skill to reestablish SQL effectively with no trouble First and preeminent thing which a client is required to do is to pass judgment on whether there is a requirement for an outside SQL reestablishing database apparatus or not. Expert assistance in the state of a SQL Server recuperation apparatus is required in the event that the client is getting any of the above mistakes on the grounds that all things considered recuperation is just conceivable by utilizing an outside programming item SysTools SQL recuperation programming can fix SQL server 2005 and 2000 database records effectively with no trouble.

SQL Web Hosting

Web Hosting is help given by an organization that leases server space to organizations or people that have website pages they need to show on the web. Web hosts give the fundamental data transmission and innovation to enable web clients to get to these site pages. While anybody can make a site page, exceptional servers devoted to web availability and facilitating are required to make the site page dynamic.

In this manner, SQL web facilitating is help that permits SQL databases to be facilitated on the web. SQL web facilitating can be utilized to store database data on the web , permit offsite individual to get to database the executives devices and give point by point data to clients or customers, commonplace applications that utilization SQL databases are ERP (Enterprise Resource Planning) and CRM (Customer Relationship Management) programs.

Things to Look for in a Quality SQL Web Hosting Service

When you've chosen to go with a SQL web have, you'll have to choose an assistance. There are a great deal of suppliers right now available; and once in a while it's hard to disclose to them separated. A quality SQL web facilitating administration should offer you the accompanying:

- Reliability
- Control Panel Options

- Technical Support
- Customer Support
- Multiple Hosting Plans

In general, on the off chance that you plan on keeping up a database online your best alternative is to go with a web facilitating administration that has servers devoted explicitly to SQL applications. Doing so will guarantee that you get the most incentive out of your venture. SQL web facilitating may cost somewhat more than standard facilitating, however it merits each penny.

CHAPTER TWELVE

Networking

NETWORKING

A network is a gathering of PCs; printers, and different gadgets that are associated together with links. The sharing of information and assets. Data goes over the links, permitting system clients to trade archives and information with one another, print to similar printers, and for the most part share any equipment or programming that is associated with the system. Every PC, printer, or other fringe gadget that is associated with the system is known as a hub. Systems can have tens, thousands, or even a large number of hubs.

Cabling:

The two most prevalent kinds of system cabling are curved pair (otherwise called 10BaseT) and thin coax (otherwise called 10Base2).10BaseT cabling looks like normal phone wire, then again, actually it has 8 wires inside rather than 4. Thin coax resembles the copper coaxial cabling that is frequently used to interface a VCR to a TV set.

Network Adapter:

A network PC is associated with the network cabling with a network interface card, (likewise called a "NIC", or network adapter). Some NICs are introduced within a

PC: the PC is opened up and a network card is connected legitimately to one of the PC's interior extension openings. 286, 386, and numerous 486 PCs have 16-piece openings, so a 16-piece NIC is required. Quicker PCs, similar to fast 486s and Pentiums, frequently have 32-piece or PCI spaces. These PCs requires 32-piece NICs to accomplish the quickest systems administration speeds feasible for speed-basic applications like work area video, sight and sound, distributing, and databases. What's more, if a PC will be utilized with a Fast Ethernet arrange, it will require a network adapter that supports 100Mbps information speeds too.

Hubs:

The last bit of the network administration astound is known as a hub. A hub is a crate that is utilized to assemble gatherings of PCs at a focal area with 10BaseT cabling. In case you're organizing a little gathering of PCs together, you might have the option to get by with a hub, some 10BaseT links, and a bunch of network adapters. Bigger systems regularly utilize a thin coax "spine" that associates a line of 10BaseT hubs together. Every hub, thus, may interface a bunch of PC together utilizing 10BaseT cabling, which enables you to assemble systems of tens, hundreds, or thousands of hubs.

Like network cards, hubs are accessible in both standard (10Mbps) and Fast Ethernet (100Mbps) forms.

LANs (Local Area Networks)

A network is any gathering of autonomous PCs that speak with each other over a common system medium. LANs are arranges normally restricted to a geographic territory, for example, a solitary structure or a school grounds. LANs can be little, connecting as few as three PCs, yet regularly interface many PCs utilized by a large number of individuals. The advancement of standard systems administration conventions and media has brought about overall expansion of LANs all through business and instructive associations.

WANs (Wide Area Networks)

Frequently a network is situated in different physical spots. Wide area networking consolidates different LANs that are geologically discrete. This is cultivated by interfacing the various LANs utilizing administrations, for example, committed rented telephone lines, dial-up telephone lines (both synchronous and asynchronous], satellite connections, and information bundle bearer administrations. Wide area networking can be as basic as a modem and remote access server for representatives to dial into, or it very well may be as intricate as several branch workplaces all around connected utilizing exceptional steering conventions and channels to limit the cost of sending information sent over huge separations.

Internet:

The Internet is an arrangement of connected systems that are worldwide in degree and encourage information correspondence administrations, for example, remote login, record move, electronic mail, the World Wide Web and newsgroups.

With the brilliant ascent popular for availability, the Internet has turned into an interchanges roadway for many clients. The Internet was at first confined to military and scholarly establishments yet now it is an undeniable course for all types of data and trade. Web sites presently give individual, instructive, political and monetary assets to each edge of the planet.

Intranet

With the headways made in program based programming for the Internet, numerous private associations are executing intranets. An intranet is a private system using Internet-type apparatuses, yet accessible just inside that association. For huge associations, an intranet gives a simple access mode to corporate data for representatives.

Ethernet

Ethernet is the most prevalent physical layer LAN innovation being used today. Other LAN types incorporate Token Ring, Fast Ethernet, Fiber Distributed Data Interface (FDDI), Asynchronous Transfer Mode (ATM) and LocalTalk. Ethernet is prominent on the grounds that it finds some kind of harmony between speed, cost and simplicity of establishment. These advantages, joined with wide acknowledgment in the PC commercial center and the capacity to help practically all famous system conventions, make Ethernet a perfect systems administration innovation for most PC clients today. The Institute for Electrical and Electronic Engineers (IEEE) characterizes the Ethernet standard as IEEE Standard 802.3.This standard characterizes rules for designing an Ethernet organize just as determining how components in an Ethernet system connect with each other. By clinging to the IEEE standard, organize gear and system conventions can convey proficiently.

Protocols:

Network protocols are benchmarks that enable PCs to impart. A protocol characterizes how PCs distinguish each other on a network, the structure that the information should take in travel, and how this data is handled once it arrives at its last goal. Protocols likewise characterizes systems for dealing with lost or harmed transmissions or "bundles." TCP/IP (for UNIX, Windows NT, Windows 95 and different stages), IPX (for Novell NetWare), DECnet (for networking Digital Equipment Corp. PCs), AppleTalk (for Macintosh PCs), and NetBIOS/NetBEUI (for LAN Manager and Windows NT networks) are the fundamental kinds of network protocols being used today.

Albeit each network protocol is unique, they all offer the equivalent physical cabling. This regular technique for getting to the physical network enables different protocols to gently exist together over the network media, and enables the developer of a network to utilize basic equipment for an assortment of protocols. This idea is known as "protocol autonomy," which implies that gadgets that are perfect at the physical and information connection layers enable the client to run a wide range of protocols over a similar medium.

Private IP address

The IP or Internet Protocol address, for example, 192.168.10.1 is a particular location used by PCs for PC networks in the correspondence and recognizable proof procedure. It is the identifier for perceiving electronic gadgets associated with a network.

The IP address 192.168.10.10 is an individual IPv4 one. It is situated somewhere in the range of 192.168.0.0 and 192.168.255.255.You can design any brands of network switches or PCs on nearby networks for utilizing it. Be that as it may, the location is limited to a solitary gadget on the network for anticipating address clashes.

Private locations are very abnormal as they can be utilized commonly for a scope of networks. It implies that having a similar IP address for an assortment of networks simultaneously doesn't bring on any obstructions or clashes. Furthermore, notwithstanding that, the scope of private IP delivers is viewed as non-routable which means these addresses are not ready to convey on the Internet as switches are set to hinder the section traffic conveyed through private locations. This might be their drawback yet it may be a bit of leeway in another manner. As external networks don't associate with private ones, this IP address won't be defenseless against the terrible components, for example, reckless or awful clients.

In the event that there is a need to connection to external networks, this private location needs to do a portal, with the goal that different networks can identify it. A switch may likewise permit the Internet use between these the two networks. So as to have this occur, you need an intermediary server or NAT (Network Address Translation]. In any occasion note that two networks may have a similar IP address. Likewise some excitement issues in getting to the switch are conceivable. Program settings should be cleared for that.

The Internet Protocol (IP) address is an elite location utilized by PCs for a PC network in the recognizable proof and correspondence forms. It is utilized as an identifier to perceive electronic gadgets associated on a network. Subsequently every gadget is exposed to a novel location.

WIRELESS LANS WLAN
COMPARING WLAN to a LAN

The predominant IEEE 802 gatherings are 802.3 and 802.11

Notwithstanding, there are significant contrasts between the two

Radio Frequency has no limits like a wire so information edges travel to anybody that can get Radio Frequency signals. Radio Frequency is un-shielded from outside sign.

Radio Frequency has some remarkable difficulties, the further from the source the flimsier the transmission.

Radio Frequency groups are controlled contrastingly in various nations. In a remote topology, a remote AP can be utilized rather than a switch.

WLANs hosts fight for access to the Radio Frequency media.

802.11 uses impact shirking rather than Collision discovery.

WLANs utilize an alternate casing design than Ethernet LANs.

WLANs require extra information in the L2.

WLANs raise protection issues since RF can reach outside the office.

Introduction TO WIRELESS LANs

802.11 LANs stretch out the 802.3 framework to give extra network alternatives

Requires extra parts and protocols

In 802.3 the switch is the AP for customers

In 802.11 customers utilize a remote adapter to get to a remote switch or AP

When associated remote customers can get to assets similarly as though they were wired

WLAN STANDARDS

802.11 uses the unlicensed modern, logical, medical(ISM) frequencies for the physical and MAC sub layer.

Mid 802.11 was 2 MBs @ 2.4 GHz

Norms improved with 11a, 11b, 11g, and 11n

802.11a&g = 54MBs

802.11b = 11MBs

802.11n seem to have a rate more prominent than 100Mbs.

OFDM is quicker and more costly to execute than DSSS

802.11a

OFDM 5GHz, less inclined to impedance, littler receiving wires

Poor range and execution vulnerable to deterrents

802.11b and g both utilize 2.4 GHz

802.11b uses DSSS

802.11g uses OFDM and DSSS   ,

2.4GHz has better range and not as effectively deterred, yet at the same time inclined to impedance

802.11n

Improves information and range without new RF band utilizes different information multi yield (IMMO) innovation

Hypothetical 248MBs

Expected to be confirmed by sept 08

RF groups distributed by ITU-R

Groups managed by the FCC, CRTC

Wi-Fi Certification

Wi-Fi cert is given by the Wi-Fi

Models guarantee interoperability

Three key associations affecting WLAN measures are

ITU-R: distributes RF groups

IEEE: indicates how RF is regulated

Wi-Fi Alliance: between compactness crosswise over sellers

The Wi-Fi partnership guarantees each of the 3 IEEE 802.11 models just as IEEE drafts and the WPA WPA2 benchmarks dependent on 802.11i.

Wireless NICs :

Early remote NICs were cards PCMCIA yet are incorporated with workstations now

PCI and USB Nics are accessible also

WIRELESS ACCESS POINTS

Customers don't normally convey straightforwardly to each

AN AP associates customers to wired LAN and changes over TCP-IP packets from 802.11 to 802.3 casings.

Customers must connect with an AP to acquire net administrations. An AP is a L2 gadget that capacities like an Ethernet hub. Radio Frequency is a common medium simply like early Ethernet transports. Gadgets that need to utilize the medium must fight for it. Remote NIC's can't recognize impacts, so all things being equal they should maintain a strategic distance from them.

Importance of Wireless Encryption

Wireless networks are all over the place. You'll see them in airports, trains, cafe's, organizations, homes, and numerous different spots. Shoppers ordinarily work with delicate information on the web, for example, money related records, medicinal records, and touchy messages. Since wireless networks have turned out to be so normal, it's important to comprehend why you ought to scramble your association just as the dangers that surface when you leave your wireless network unbound. In the domain of networking, there are numerous vectors for assault on open wireless networks. It is generously simpler for somebody to increase unapproved access to your PC and records on the off chance that they are on your network with you. Also, it is conceivable that the aggressor will break down the traffic on your network, enabling him to perceive what locales you visit and to possibly take your accreditations for different destinations. Different dangers you face are less genuine, yet at the same time irritating and hard to alleviate. The assailant on your network may decide not to access your PC or examine your traffic, however rather play out a disavowal of administration assault. This sort of assault floods the network (or simply your PC if that is the situation) with solicitations, making it fantastically troublesome and much of the time difficult to get to the web and network.

Setting up your wireless network to fuse encryption isn't hard, and as a rule will just take a couple of minutes. Each wireless switch has an alternate technique to change the settings for your network, and once you realize how to get to those settings, it's a matter of a couple of snaps and composing in a secret key. WEP encryption ought to never be utilized to encrypt a wireless network. The encryption can be split effectively with the correct tools and generally in under 3 minutes. WPA and WPA2 are right now the best decisions for wireless encryption; WPA2 being the better choice of the two.

Port Scanning:

What is port filtering you may ask? Everything considered, port filtering can be portray various ways, anyway on a very basic level is the show of sending packs to an objective of social occasion of hosts to endeavor to get a response. For what reason do I need to port yield and do others port scope me? You should port scope your broadband relationship with see what your network has open to the web and others may port yield you to find a course into your network. Port looking at should be workable for substantial avocations and noxious purposes. Other certifiable substantial defenses for port filtering is to see what ports your item may use this can empower you to research network issues. There are such countless inspirations to list here on the virtuosos of ports breadths and port yield programming yet you ought to at first understand what a port is and how it impacts your PC and network.

What is a port and how can it work?

Ports are like locations for instance in the event that you send a bundle to a companion you should put numerous sections on the delivery mark for it to get to him. You would require a name, road number, city, State, postal division, and once in a while a nation. Without this data your bundle would not get the beneficiary. Ports work likewise. Ports are a piece of the location for web traffic. Ports likewise must have other information to be utilized like an IP address, Protocol, and transport media.

Who controls port numbers?

Ports numbers are institutionalized however the "Web Assigned Numbers Authority" or IANA. The port numbers are isolated into three territories: The Well Known Ports, Registered Ports, and the Dynamic and additionally Private Ports.

The Well Known Ports are those from 0 through 1023. DCCP Well Known ports SHOULD NOT be utilized without IANA enrollment. The enrollment methodology is characterized in [RFC4340], Section 19.9.

The Registered Ports are those from 1024 through 49151 DCCP Registered ports SHOULD NOT be utilized without IANA enrollment. The enrollment methodology is characterized in [RFC4340], Section 19.9.

The Dynamic and additionally Private Ports are those from 49152 through 65535.

Port Scanning Software

How about we currently investigate programming that is utilized for port checking. A great deal of the product out there for port filtering additionally has different prospects for defenselessness examining. One of the most notable port checking devices is NMAP.

Nmap ("Network Mapper") is a free open source utility for network investigation or security inspecting. It was intended to quickly examine huge networks, despite the fact that it works fine against single hosts. Nmap utilizes crude IP packets in novel manners to figure out what hosts are accessible on the network, what administrations (application name and form) those hosts are offering, what working frameworks (and OS renditions) they are running, what kind of bundle filters/firewalls are being used, and many different attributes. Nmap keeps running on most sorts of PCs and both reassure and graphical forms are accessible. Nmap is free and open source (portrayal from NMAP's site).

Angry IP scanner is a quick IP scanner and port scanner. It can examine IP addresses in any range just as any their ports. Its twofold document size is exceptionally little contrasted with other IP or port scanners. Irate IP scanner essentially pings every IP address to check on the off chance that it's alive, at that point alternatively it is settling its hostname, decides the MAC address, examines ports, and so forth. The measure of assembled information about each host can be reached out with the accessible module's (portrayal from angryziber.com).

SuperScan 4 is a Powerful TCP port scanner and resolver. Here are a portion of the fates; Superior examining speed, Support for boundless IP ranges, Improved host identification utilizing different ICMP techniques, TCP SYN checking, UDP filtering (two strategies), IP address import supporting extents and CIDR groups, Simple HTML report age, Source port filtering, Fast hostname settling, Extensive standard snatching, Massive implicit port rundown portrayal database, IP and port sweep request randomization, A determination of helpful tools (ping, follow course, Whois, and so forth.). SuperScan is from foundstone.com and this portrayal was assembled from that point site.

Online Scanners

There are additionally sites that offer free port sweeps to enable you to verify your network. Here is a rundown of a couple of examining locales.

Sygate Online Scan (scan.sygate.com) expanded security check (Stealth Scan, Trojan Scan.

Planet Security Firewall-Check (planet-security.net) Fast, expanded check, checks right now high-jeopardized ports.

Crucialtests (crucialtests.com) compact, incl. counsel.

ShieldsUP (grc.com) Quick Scanner, obviously spread out.

How to block all the scanning

Since you have seen what ports examining is and the utilizations for it you should realize how to shield you network from sweeps. The best activity is have a firewall and utilize around date Anti-infection and Anti-Spyware programs. You won't have the option to stop the outputs on your network however with a decent firewall the individual examining you won't perceive any traffic back and ideally expect your association isn't on or no amass.

How a Port Scan Works

With numerous new security dangers showing up each day, ensuring your PC and computerized records is considerably progressively important. One risk today is port filtering. Port examining happens to the vast majority whether they understand it or not. Ensuring yourself against port sweeps can enable you to verify your framework from vindictive clients.

All PCs have ports, and administrations keep running on these ports. At the point when your PC needs to associate with your mail server so as to browse your email, it will open one of these ports and make an association with download your new email. Anyway now and then these ports are consistently on and tuning in. A port sweep happens when attacker examines a host to see which ports are open and which are shut or not being used.

Think about a port output like checking entryways and windows of your home to check whether it is bolted or not. While, the attacker may not break into your home he may realize that there is a window opened and section can be accomplished effectively. A port scanner works similarly as it checks ports on your PC to see which is shut or open. It isn't illicit in many spots to do a port output in light of the fact that you're simply checking if the association can be made and not really making an association with the host. Anyway it is conceivable to make a Denial of Service assault if port sweeps are made more than once.

Numerous firewalls can secure you against port sweeps. A firewall is a program that screens active and approaching associations with your PC. A firewall may open all ports on your framework to adequately prevent filters from demonstrating any ports. While this methodology works much of the time. Port Scans have progressed with new systems, for example, ICMP port inaccessible sweeps and NULL outputs. While it's ideal to attempt to filter every single port sweep to your PC, it's additionally important to understand that any ports that are open and listening should be explored. Leaving open ports on your machine can prompt a framework bargain causing lost information, and perhaps fraud. Your very own port output framework can indicate you precisely what an attacker sees and what kind of move you have to make to avert an assault on your framework.

One of the most prominent port scanners accessible today is NMap from insecure.org. NMap is accessible for nothing download and is accessible for UNIX and Windows based frameworks. It's important to see how NMap functions so you can adopt a similar strategy as an attacker would against you. There are other port examining programming accessible and every ha their own port checking highlights. Be that as it may, NMap is by a wide margin the most mainstream and is stacked with highlights, and various sorts of port sweeps you can perform.

Detecting Network Sniffers

A network sniffer is a program or tool that listens in on network traffic and assembles information from packets. In some cases such wiretaps are completed by the network manager for advantageous purposes (like interruption location, execution investigation, and so on.). Then again, malevolent gatecrashers may introduce packet sniffers so as to recover clear-content usernames and passwords from the neighborhood network or other essential data transmitted on the network. Defenseless protocols (with clear-content passwords) incorporate telnet, pop3, imap, ftp, smtp-auth and NNTP. Sniffers work since Ethernet was intended to be shared. Most networks use communicate innovation - messages for one PC can be perused by another PC on that network. By and by, PCs overlook messages with the exception of those that were sent legitimately to them (or communicate to all hosts on the network). In any case, PCs can be put in wanton mode and made to acknowledge messages regardless of whether they are not implied for them - this is the way a Sniffer works.

Individuals accept that PCs associated with a switch are protected from sniffing — yet this isn't so. PCs associated with switches are similarly as defenseless against sniffers as those associated with a hub.

How a Sniffer functions

A PC associated with a LAN has 2 locations - one is the MAC address that exceptionally recognizes every hub in a network and which is put away on the network card. The MAC address is utilized by the Ethernet protocol when building edges to move information. The other is the IP address, which is utilized by applications. The Data Link (layer 2 of the OSI model) utilizes an Ethernet header with the MAC address of the goal machine. The Network (layer 3 of the OSI model) is in charge of mapping IP network delivers to the MAC address as required by the Data Link Protocol. Layer 3 endeavors to look-into the MAC address of the goal machine in a table, called the ARP store. In the event that no MAC passage is found for the IP address, the Address Resolution Protocol communicates a solicitation packet (ARP request) to all machines on the network. The machine with that IP address reacts to the source machine with its MAC address. This MAC address at that point gets added to the source machines ARP Cache. This MAC address is then utilized by the source machine in the entirety of its interchanges with the goal machine.

There are two essential sorts of Ethernet conditions - shared and exchanged. In a common Ethernet condition all hosts are associated with a similar transport and rival each other for data transmission. In such a domain packets implied for one machine are gotten by the various machines. Every one of the PCs on the mutual Ethernet contrast the edge's goal MAC address and their own. On the off chance that the two don't coordinate, the casing is unobtrusively disposed of. A machine running a sniffer defies this guideline and acknowledges all casings. Such a machine is said to have been placed into unbridled mode and can viably tune in to all the traffic on the network. Sniffing in a mutual Ethernet condition is aloof and, subsequently, hard to distinguish.

In an exchanged situation, the hosts are associated with a switch rather than a hub. The switch keeps up a table that monitors every PC's MAC address and the physical port on the change to which that MAC address is associated. The switch is a clever gadget which sends bundles just to the goal PC. Subsequently, the way toward placing a machine into indiscriminate mode to accumulate packets doesn't work. In any case, this doesn't imply that exchanged networks are secure and can't be sniffed.

Despite the fact that a switch is more secure than a hub, you can utilize the accompanying strategies to sniff on a switch:

ARP spoofing– the ARP is stateless for example you can send an ARP answer regardless of whether none has not been requested, and such an answer will be acknowledged. For instance, one method is to ARP parody the portal of the network. The ARP reserve of the focused on host will presently have an off-base section for the portal and is said to be harmed. Starting here on, all the traffic bound for the door will go through the sniffer machine. Another stunt that can be utilized is to harm a hosts ARP reserve by setting the doors MAC address to ARP store by setting the portals MAC address to FF:FF:FF:FF:FF:FF(also known as the communicate MAC).

MAC Flooding– switches keep an interpretation table that maps MAC delivers to physical ports on the switch. This enables them to wisely course packets starting with one host then onto the next. The switch has a restricted measure of memory for this work. The MAC flooding utilizes this restriction to barrage a switch with phony MAC addresses until the switch can't keep up. The switch at that point goes into what is known as a 'bomb open mode', so, all things considered it starts going about as a hub by communicating bundles to every one of the machines on the network. When that happens sniffing can be performed effectively.

Detecting Sniffers on the Network

A sniffer is normally passive - it just gathers information and is particularly hard to identify when running in a common Ethernet condition. In any case, it is anything but difficult to identify a sniffer when introduced on an exchanged network. At the point when introduced on a PC a sniffer generates some limited quantity of traffic - which considers its location utilizing the accompanying kinds of procedures:

Ping Method- a ping solicitation is sent with the IP address of the speculate machine however not its MAC address. In a perfect world, no one should see this. Bundle as every Ethernet adapter will dismiss it as it doesn't coordinate its MAC address. Be that as it may, if the speculate machine is running a sniffer it will react since it acknowledges all bundles.

ARP Method- this strategy depends on the reality all machines store ARPs (for example MAC addresses). Here, we send a no communicated ARP so just machines in unbridled mode will store our ARP address. Next, we send a communicate ping bundle with our IP, yet an alternate MAC address. Just a machine which has our right MAC address from the sniffed ARP casing will have the option to react to our broadcast ping request.

On Local Host- if a machine has been undermined a programmer may have left a sniffer running. There are utility projects that can be run which report whether the neighborhood machine's network adapter has been set to promiscuous mode.

Latency Method- depends on the suspicion most sniffers do some sort of parsing, in this way expanding the heap on that machine. In this manner it will require some investment to react to a ping packet. This distinction accordingly times can be utilized as a pointer of whether a machine is in promiscuous mode or not.

ARP Watch- to keep a programmer from ARP spoofing the portal there are utilities that can be utilized to screen the ARP reserve of a machine to check whether there is duplication for a machine.

Step by step instructions to Protect against Sniffing

The most ideal approach to verify a network against sniffing is to utilize encryption. While this won't keep sniffers from working, it will guarantee the information gathered by sniffers is uninterpretable. Likewise, on an exchanged network, the odds are ARP spoofing will be utilized for sniffing purposes. The machine that the programmer will undoubtedly ARP-spoof is the default gateway. To keep this from happening it is recommended the MAC address of the gateway be for all time added to each host's ARP cache.

Use SSH rather than telnet.

Use HTTPS rather than HTTP (if the site supports it).

Whenever worried about email security, attempt a help, for example, Hushmail (www.hushmail.com), which uses SSL to guarantee that information isn't perused in travel. Additionally, Pretty Good Privacy (www.gnupg.org) can be utilized for encrypting and marking messages to keep others from understanding them.

Utilize a sniffer detector. For instance, the product bundle PromiScan is viewed as the standard sniffing node discovery tool and is suggested by the SANS (SysAdmin, Audit, Network, Security) Institute. It is an application bundle used to remotely screen PCs on neighborhood networks to find network interfaces working in promiscuous mode.

How to Dodge ARP Poisoning

A Successful ARP poisoning is undetectable to the client. Since the end client is uninformed of ARP poisoning he will peruse the, web ordinarily while the attacker is gathering information from the session. The information gathered might be passwords, banking records, messages and sites. This is known as "Man in the Middle Attack."

How does this occur? The attacker sends poisoned ARP request to the gateway router device. The gateway router is presently mentally programmed, to imagine that the course to any PC through the Subnet needs to go through the attackers PC. Then again, all hosts on the subnet feel that the attacker PC/MAC is the genuine gateway and they send all traffic and data to this PC. Be that as it may, the attacker PC advances this information to the gateway.

In this manner there is one attacker PC that sees all traffic on the network. Also, if this assault is gone for one single PC the attacker can simply Spoof this unfortunate casualties PC to his own and just impact on the network. The attackers PC must be truly quick as the gateway has huge steering tables and numerous sessions are running in parallel. Most ordinary PCs can't deal with a huge inflow of information and this makes the network stop or crash. This occurs as the attackers PC isn't good enough and the number of packets have dropped as the PC can't stay aware of the progression of enormous volumes of information.

A great many people are biased to feel that utilizing a PC from the sheltered corner of their house is the best alternative. Here is some news for them, until and except if you don't have a firewall introduced on the web association, there is constantly a threat of spoofing of outbound information from your home PC. In the event that you are utilizing wireless, it is important to encrypt it, else you would draw undue consideration from attackers. So as to forestall a programmer structure spoofing the portal there are different utilities that can be utilized to screen the ARP Cache of a machine to check whether, there is any duplication for a machine.

Be that as it may, the most ideal approach to verify a network against sniffing is encryption. Presently, you will be unable to prevent attackers from sniffing, yet the information that they get would be made uninterpretable. Additionally, on an exchanged network, the odds of ARP spoofing would be utilized for sniffing purposes.

Useful Links

https://inteltechniques.com
    https://osintframework.com
    https://owasp.org
    https://evilzone.org
    https://hackforums.net
    https://pastebin.com
    https://www.exploit-db.com
    https://www.hackthissite.org
    www.itsecgames.com
    https://www.offensive-security.com